The Perfect PAIR!

Purses, Handbags and Wallets for All Occasions

by Marne Ventura

raintree

a Capstone company — publishers for children

Raintree is an imprint of Capstone Global Library Limited, a company incorporated in England and Wales having its registered office at 264 Banbury Road, Oxford, OX2 7DY – Registered company number: 6695582

www.raintree.co.uk
myorders@raintree.co.uk

Edited by Mari Bolte and Alesha Sullivan
Designed by Tracy Davies McCabe
Photos by Karon Dubke
Original photos © Capstone Global Library Limited 2017
Picture Research by Morgan Walters
Production by Kathy McColley
Originated by Capstone Global Library Limited
Printed and bound in China.

ISBN 978 1 4747 2389 3
20 19 18 17 16
10 9 8 7 6 5 4 3 2 1

British Library Cataloguing in Publication Data
A full catalogue record for this book is available from the British Library.

Acknowledgements:
We would like to thank the following for permission to reproduce effects: Shutterstock: ganpanjanee, design element, Ozerina Anna, design element, Stephanie Zieber, design element, Vaclav Mach, design element, Yellowj, design element

Every effort has been made to contact copyright holders of material reproduced in this book. Any omissions will be rectified in subsequent printings if notice is given to the publisher.

CONTENTS

It's in the BAG

THE PERFECT BAG IS, WELL, PERFECT!

Whether you're walking to school, packing for a sleepover or meeting friends in town, you need your hands free and your belongings safe.

It's fun to carry a bag made with just the right fabric, a pop of colour or some flashy beads. The stripes on your purse and the lace on your backpack show your special style. By learning to make your own bags, you can create a look that's uniquely yours.

You'll be surprised at how easy it is to make your own handbags, purses and wallets. Start with an inexpensive bag and decorate it with stamps and ruffles. Upcycle an old handbag with paint or a glam chain handle. Have craft or sewing supplies on hand? Stitch together a coin purse or create your own sleepover tote. With each project you complete, you'll improve your crafting skills, have loads of fun and add a cute bag to your collection.

WHILE YOU CAN USE A SEWING MACHINE IN MANY OF THESE PROJECTS, SEWING BY HAND WILL WORK JUST AS WELL. HERE ARE SOME BASIC STITCHES USED IN THE BOOK:

1. **Tacking stitch:** A tacking stitch is a longer-than-usual straight stitch. Sometimes tacking is used instead of pins, to hold fabric together until it's sewn with a smaller stitch. Tacking stitches are perfect for making ruffles, because when you pull the end of the thread, it causes the fabric to gather.

2. **Backstitch:** A backstitch is similar to an ordinary straight stitch but it looks more like a solid line. You insert your needle down through the middle of the last stitch and come up right after that stitch.

3. **Running stitch:** A running stitch usually resembles a dashed line, with short stitches that won't pucker or fall loose. Bring up the needle from the underside and then down again a bit over and keep repeating.

4. **Topstitch:** Topstitch is a row of straight stitches that are used as a decorative feature.

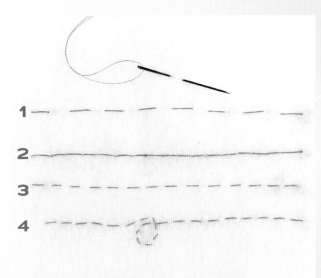

MATERIALS:

plain canvas bag
fabric
fabric scissors
pins

2.5-cm-(1-inch-) wide
   grosgrain ribbon
fabric glue

Fun ruffle TOTE

Need a tote to hold your gear? Don't get ruffled. (Or do!)
Fill your frilly tote and you're on your way wherever.

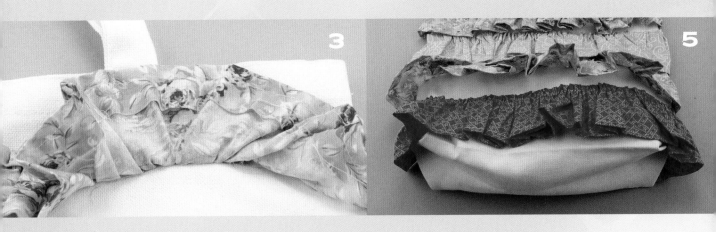

1. Measure the opening of the bag. Multiply by 3. Cut a strip of 10.2-centimetre- (4-inch-) wide fabric to this length. Sew the two short ends together to form a circular strip.

2. Fold under one long edge 0.6 centimetres (¼ inch) towards the wrong side. Fold over again and stitch in place.

3. Sew a tacking stitch 0.6 centimetres (¼ inch) from the other long edge. Repeat 1.3 centimetres (½ inch) from the edge.

4. Pin the strip evenly around the top of the bag, with the raw edge 2.5 centimetres (1 inch) from the top. Pull the ends of the two top tacking threads to make the fabric gather into a ruffle.

5. Sew the ruffle in place along the tacking threads.

Tip: When cutting fabric, a pair of fabric scissors (or shears) is best. A pair of scissors made for cutting paper won't work as well; They have handles that are the same size. On a pair of fabric scissors, one handle is often much larger than the other. This allows you to hold the scissors with several fingers in the handle. Additionally, fabric scissors are much sharper and able to easily cut through thick material.

MATERIALS:

fine sandpaper
old leather bag
rubbing alcohol
painter's tape

acrylic paint and paintbrush
sticky-back jewels
    and embellishments
clear acrylic spray sealant

Rock a colour BLOCK

What says "happy" better than a pop of colour?
This dressed-up bag is the perfect way to jazz up a
standard leggings-and-tee combo.

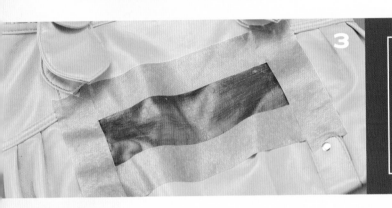

> *Tip: For maximum flair, choose bright, contrasting colours like purple and orange or turquoise and yellow.*

1. Sand the section of the leather bag you would like to paint. The surface needs to be rough so the paint will stick.

2. Wipe the bag with a clean cloth to remove any residue. Wipe again with a cloth dampened with rubbing alcohol.

3. Mask the edges of the sanded section with painter's tape.

4. Use a mixture of half paint and half water to paint the section.

5. When the section is almost dry, apply a second coat.

6. Continue steps 4 and 5 until you are happy with the colour. Let dry, then remove tape.

7. Use sticky-back jewels and embellishments to decorate the bag.

8. Spray the entire bag with an acrylic sealant. Let dry before using.

MATERIALS:

fabric with large,
  simple designs
vinyl zip purse
fabric decoupage glue
  and foam brush

clear acrylic spray sealant
4 mm to 6 mm glass beads
head pin
pliers
6-mm split ring

Decoupage PURSE

For occasions that don't call for a handbag, a super cute purse is just the thing. Don't search everywhere for that special, just-your-style purse. Do it yourself with decoupage!

7

Tip: Find cool designs on vintage clothes or pillowcases at car boot sales and charity shops.

1. Cut out the designs from the fabric. Cover the purse with decoupage glue and press the fabric onto the purse. Let dry.

2. Cover the purse with another coat of decoupage glue. Repeat for a glossier look.

3. When the decoupage is completely dry, spray the purse with acrylic sealant.

4. For the zip pull, arrange the beads on a head pin. Leave 1.3 centimetres (½ inch) of wire at the top.

5. Use pliers to twist the end of the head pin into a loop.

6. Attach a split ring to the loop.

7. Use the split ring to connect the beaded pull to the zip.

Glam HANDBAG

Got an old bag with worn-out handles? Don't just toss it! Dress it up with a trendy new handle made of gold chain and colourful leather.

MATERIALS:

wire cutter
purse with damaged handles,
  connected with metal rings
1.8 metres (6 feet) of 10-mm
  by 7-mm chain

7.3 metres (24 feet) of 3-mm
  suede lace
hot glue and hot glue gun
4 jump rings
round-nosed jewellery pliers

1. Use the wire cutter to remove the bag's handles. Cut four lengths of chain the same length as the old handles.

2. Cut two pieces of suede lace that are 3 times the length of one chain.

3. Lay two chains side-by-side and thread a piece of lace through the top rings.

4. Wrap the ends of the lace under the chains and through the next chain links. Cross the lace and weave it through the next chain links. Continue weaving over and under so that the laces form Xs that join the two chains together.

5. At the end of the chain, knot and trim the lace. Glue the ends down with hot glue.

6. Use the jump rings to attach the handle to the bag.

7. Repeat steps 3–6 to make a second handle.

Tip: Craft and discount shops sell inexpensive jewellery starter kits that include wire cutters, round-nosed pliers and an assortment of head pins and jump rings.

MATERIALS:

brown paper bag
dinner plate with a 30.5-cm
  (12-inch) diameter
marker
scissors

sponge
brown acrylic paint
metallic acrylic paint
adhesive studs and flowers
clear acrylic spray sealant

Brown bag CLUTCH

Celebrate Earth Day every day with an eco-friendly project. Repurpose a brown paper bag into an envelope-style clutch. You'll reduce the rubbish in the landfill and look great in the process.

1. Gently pull off the bag handles (if any) and discard. Turn the bag inside out so the printing doesn't show.

2. Flatten the bag and fold it in half horizontally.

3. Place the plate on the bag. The edges of the plate should line up with the top corners of the bag. Trace around the plate. Unfold the bag and cut around the trace lines to create a flap for your clutch.

4. Re-fold the bag, and tuck the flap inside.

5. Use a sponge and brown paint to give the outside of the clutch a leather-like look. Add layers of metallic paint to give the colours more depth.

6. Stick jewels and flowers along the edge of the flap.

7. Spray acrylic sealant over the entire bag. Let dry completely before using.

Tip: Crumple the bag with your hands to make it look even more like leather.

Pocket TOTE

A crafty girl just can't have enough totes. Whatever your hobby – sewing, beading, painting – you need to keep your supplies together while you're at home. This tote looks pretty while it keeps your project organized and portable.

FOR THE HANDLES:

1. Measure one of the bag's handles. Add 2.5 centimetres (1 inch) to the width and length. Cut a length of fabric to this size.

2. Fold the sides of the fabric under 1.3 centimetres (½ inch) and iron in place. Pin the folds to the handle. Sew along each edge. Repeat for the second handle.

FOR THE POCKET:

1. Cut a piece of fabric 20.3 by 28 centimetres (8 by 11 inches). Place the fabric on the tote as desired. Sew the two sides and the bottom of the fabric to the tote to make a pocket.

2. Measure and cut the ribbon into four pieces that are long enough to trim the fabric pocket.

3. Sew or glue the ribbon along the outside of the fabric. (Make sure you don't sew the pocket shut.) Trim the tassels from the side pieces of trim, if desired.

Tip: Tassels not your thing? Make a monogram with black buttons on the pocket instead.

MATERIALS:

fabric place mat
fabric for lining
iron
pins

hook-and-loop sticky dots
hot glue and hot glue gun
silk flower or other
    embellishment

Pretty place mat CLUTCH

Got a friend with a birthday coming up? Why not surprise her with a handmade gift? Whip up this easy handbag in her favourite colour.

1. Cut the fabric 5 centimetres (2 inches) wider and longer than the place mat.

2. Fold in the long sides of the fabric 2.5 centimetres (1 inch) and iron.

3. Open the ironed edges and fold in the corners. Then refold the sides in to make smooth corners. Iron.

4. Pin the wrong side of the fabric to the wrong side of the place mat. Stitch the two pieces together about 0.3 centimetres (⅛ inch) from the edge.

5. Fold the place mat roughly into thirds vertically. The bottom fold will form the pocket. The top fold will form the flap. Sew along the sides of the bottom fold, leaving the flap free.

6. Attach one of the hook-and-loop dots under the flap and the other dot on the front of the clutch.

7. Hot glue a flower to the centre of the flap.

Tip: There's more than one way to open and close a bag! Check out your local craft or fabric shop for different fasteners. Zips, buttons, magnetic or sew-on snaps, twist locks, and glue-on or sew-on clasps are all alternative options.

Super sleepover SACK

Start with some pretty fabric, satin ribbon and a few seams. End up with a cute drawstring bag to hold your pyjamas and toiletries. Your friends won't believe you made it!

MATERIALS:

50 cm (1½ feet) of cotton fabric
iron
needle and thread or sewing machine
pins
safety pin
1 m (1 yard) white satin ribbon,
   1.9 cm (¾ inch) wide

Tip: The selvedge edge of fabric is finished by the manufacturer so it won't fray. Selvedges should be trimmed away before you begin a project because they are thicker than the rest of the fabric.

1. Trim off 5 centimetres (2 inches) of the selvedge side of the fabric.

2. Hem one long raw edge of the fabric by folding it in 1.3 centimetres (½ inch), ironing and sewing in place.

3. Fold the fabric in half vertically. On the wrong side of the fabric, sew a 1.3-centimetre (½-inch) seam across the bottom and up the side. Stop 10.2 centimetres (4 inches) before the top edge. Backstitch.

4. Fold the top edge down 5 centimetres (2 inches). Pin. Sew close to the top edge and along the lower edge to form a casing.

5. Turn the bag right-side-out. Attach a safety pin to the end of the ribbon. Push the closed safety pin into the casing and feed the ribbon through to the other side. Remove the safety pin, and tie the ends of the ribbon in a knot.

MATERIALS:

resealable snack-sized bag
needle and thread
scissors

17.8-cm (7-inch) cotton
   quilted potholder
hot glue and hot glue gun
button

Cute quilted CASE

*A mini bag is the perfect place to stash your
lip balm and hand cream. Starting with a potholder
makes this project super easy.*

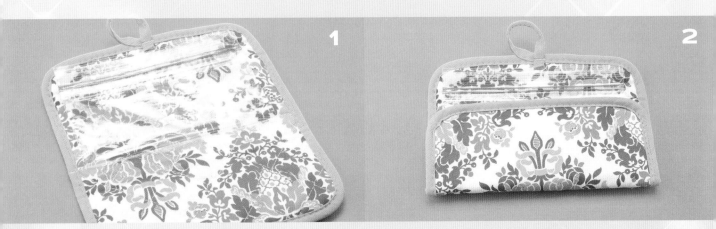

1. Place a resealable bag on top of the potholder. Sew horizontally down the middle of the bag to attach it to the potholder. Cut off the excess part of the bag.

2. Fold the potholder into thirds. The loop should be on the top flap.

3. Sew along the sides of the potholder to make a bag.

4. Fold the top third of the potholder down to form a flap.

5. Sew a button onto the front of the bag so that it lines up with the loop. If the potholder did not come with a centre loop, sew a small fabric loop in the centre of the other side.

*Tip: If you want to separate and store several items,
sew in more resealable bags.*

MATERIALS:

23-cm (9-inch) nylon zip
two 23-by-17.8-cm (9-by-
7-inch) pieces of cotton
fabric, for lining

two 23-by-17.8-cm pieces
of cotton fabric, for pouch
needle and thread or
sewing machine

Zippy pencil POUCH

Sew up this handy little bag in a sec. Then fill it with your favourite pencils and throw it in your backpack with a sketchpad.

1. Place the wrong side of the zip along the long top edge of the lining fabric. Make sure the zip touches the right side of the fabric. Place the pouch fabric over the zip, right-side-down. Use pins to hold the zip in place.

2. Stitch the zip and material in place. Use a zip foot, if you're using a sewing machine.

3. Fold the pouch and lining fabrics away from the zip.

4. Repeat steps 1 and 3 on the other side of the zip.

5. Topstitch along the edges of the fabric, close to the zip.

6. Open the zip about two-thirds of the way. (If you don't open the zip, you won't be able to turn the pouch right-side-out after it's sewn.) Place the pouch and lining fabrics right sides together. Fold the zip teeth towards the lining. Pin.

7. Sew around the edges of the pouch and lining with a 1.3-centimetre (½-inch) seam, leaving a 7.6-centimetre (3-inch) opening on the bottom edge of the lining. Clip corners and turn right-side-out.

8. Topstitch the opening in the bottom of the lining. Push the lining into the pouch and zip it up!

Tip: A zip foot is different from the all-purpose foot used for normal machine sewing. It's thinner and has a notch for the needle. This lets you sew close to the edge of the zip.

CLIPPING CURVES

To make rounded corners lay flat, make slits perpendicular to the stitches every 1.3 centimetres (½ inch) around the curve before you turn your project right-side-out. Be careful not to clip the stitches!

MATERIALS:

one pillowcase

needle and thread or
sewing machine

measuring tape

pins

Pillowy BAG

A simple bag is a sleepy step away! Use an old, well-loved pillowcase, or pick up two contrasting cases to make a matching bag for your best friend.

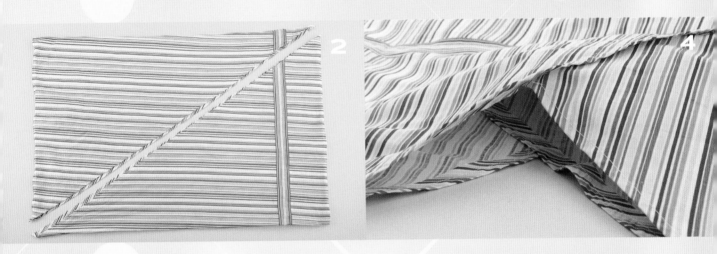

1. Trim 0.6 centimetres (¼ inch) off of the closed end of the pillowcase.

2. Cut the case in half diagonally the long way.

3. Turn under the diagonal cut edges 0.6 centimetres (¼ inch) and sew to make a narrow hem.

4. Place one pillowcase half inside the other half and line up the bottom edges. Pin and sew where the fabrics overlap in front, being careful not to sew through the back.

5. Repeat step 4 on the back side.

6. Turn the fabric inside out and sew the bottom onto the other half of the pillowcase.

7. Turn the bag right-side-out and tie the top ends with a knot to make a handle.

Tip: Pillowcases make great totes for books, sports equipment or hobby supplies. If they get dirty, you can just toss them in the washing machine.

Monogram glitter WRISTLET

Every girl needs a sparkly wristlet to hold a few pounds or an ID card. Skip the pricey boutique and make your own. Use the cuff of a shirt that's on its way to the charity shop.

MATERIALS:

scissors
old long-sleeve dress shirt
ribbon
needle and thread
  or sewing machine

seam ripper
button
washable marker
fabric glitter glue
glitter

1. Cut the cuff away from the sleeve.

2. Cut 25.4 centimetres (10 inches) of ribbon. Fold the ribbon in half to form a wrist loop. Insert the two raw edges into the side of the cuff about 2.5 centimetres (1 inch) below the button.

3. With the flap open, sew along the sides of the cuff to form a pocket.

4. Use a seam ripper to remove the old button. Replace with a fun, colourful button.

5. With the cuff buttoned, use a light washable marker to draw the shape of your initial.

6. Fill the initial with glue and sprinkle on glitter. Gently shake off extra glitter. Dry completely before using.

Tip: When throwing away damaged clothing, use a seam ripper to take off fancy buttons. Save them in a jar so you'll be ready for projects like this one.

MATERIALS:

206.5-square-centimetre
 (32-square-inch)
 fleece blanket
1.8 m (2 yards) of 2.5-cm-
 (1-inch-) wide ribbon

chalk or marker
fabric scissors
needle and thread
 or sewing machine
tape measure

Beautiful bow BAG

Start with a fleece blanket and end up with a soft bag!
Fill it with pyjamas, swimsuit or gym clothes.

1. Fold the blanket in half. Fold it in half again so that you have a corner and four layers.

2. Holding the start of the tape measure at the corner of the blanket, make marks at the 35.6-centimetre (14-inch) point every 5 centimetres (2 inches). Connect the marks to make an arc. Cut along the marks. Unfold.

3. With the circle folded in half, mark thirteen 2.5-centimetre (1-inch) lines. Make them about 7.6 centimetres (3 inches) apart and 3.8 centimetres (1.5 inches) from the edge. Cut through both sides. Open.

4. Cut the ribbon into two 1-yard (1-m) lengths.

5. Sew the ends of one ribbon to opposite sides of the circle. Centre each end between two slits. This will be the handle.

6. Thread the other ribbon in and out of the slits. Pull the ends to gather and close the bag. Tie a bow.

Tip: Fleece is easy to work with because it doesn't fray. Discount shops sell inexpensive fleece blankets. Or you could buy fleece material at a fabric shop.

MATERIALS:

fabric scissors
sequinned fabric
lining fabric
lightweight fusible
  interfacing
flannel
iron

1.3-cm- (½-inch-)
  wide ribbon
hot glue and hot
  glue gun
3 hook-and-loop
  sticky dots

Sparkly bow CLUTCH

Going to a fancy party? You'll look great carrying this shiny little bag! Slide your hand under the bow to hold it.

1. Cut a 25.4-by-23-centimetre (10-by-9 inch) rectangle from the sequinned fabric. Cut a 25.4-by-45.7-centimetre (10-by-18-inch) rectangle from the sequin fabric, the lining fabric and the interfacing.

2. Place the interfacing on the wrong side of the larger sequinned fabric rectangle. The fusible side of the interfacing should face down. Set the flannel on top of the interfacing to protect the sequins. With the iron set on low, gently fuse interfacing to the wrong side of the sequinned fabric.

3. Sew the larger sequin rectangle and the lining together with right sides facing in. Leave a 7.6-centimetre (3-inch) opening along one side. Turn right-side-out. Set the iron to low and press the lining side gently.

4. Fold the fabric from step 3 into thirds with the sequin side out. Sew along the sides to form a pocket.

5. Fold the smaller sequin fabric rectangle in half lengthwise, right-side-in. Sew along the edges, leaving a 7.6-centimetre (3-inch) opening. Turn right-side-out. Press open with your fingers or cover with a flannel and press with the iron set on low.

6. Sew the short ends of the smaller rectangle to the sides of the flap from step 4.

7. Cut a 10.2-centimetre (4-inch) length of ribbon. Pleat the centre of the smaller rectangle and wrap the ribbon around the pleat to hold in place. Use hot glue to secure the ribbon.

8. Attach the sticky dots to the centre and corners of the underside of the flap. Attach the other halves to the centre and corners of the front of the pocket.

INTERFACING

Interfacing makes fabric stiffer and thicker. Fusible interfacing has a rough side that fuses or sticks to fabric when it's ironed. To apply, place the bumpy side of the interfacing against the wrong side of the fabric, cover with a damp flannel, and press for 10 to 15 seconds. Pick up the iron and repeat until you've covered the entire piece.

MATERIALS:

scissors
tape measure
four 23-by-30.5-cm (9-by-
12-inch) sheets of craft
felt in different colours
pins

hook-and-loop sticky dots
hot glue and hot glue gun
1-cm- (⅜-inch-) wide ribbon
needle and thread or
sewing machine
button

Wacky, woolly PURSE

The purse is the heart of a bag. It keeps your cards and money safe and organized. Choose felt in wild colours for this bifold purse so you can find it fast.

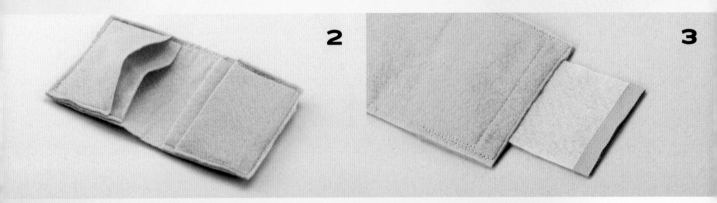

1. Cut rectangles from the felt in the following sizes:
   • outer piece: one 10.2-by-17.8-centimetre (4-by-7-inch) piece
   • inner piece: one 9.5-by-17.8-centimetre (3.75-by-7-inch) piece
   • pockets: four 9.5-by-5.7-centimetre (3.75-by-2.25-inch) pieces
   • tab: one 7-by-6.4-centimetre (2.75-by-2.5-inch) piece

2. Pin one pocket piece on the inner piece 1.3 centimetres (½ inch) from the top. Sew the side and bottom edges.

3. Overlap the next pocket piece 1.3 centimetres (½ inch) from the top of the first pocket. Sew in place along the sides and bottom edge.

4. Sew the outer piece to the inner piece, tucking the end of the tab in the middle of one side. Sew on the sides and bottom edge.

5. Attach the hook-and-loop sticky dots to the underside of the tab and the outside of the purse.

6. Hot glue ribbon to the outside edges. Sew a button to the outside of the tab.

Tip: For a more sophisticated look, use neutral colours such as black or grey. Decorate the purse and tab with strips of beaded trim instead of ribbons and a button.

Denim and lace
BACKPACK

Make an everyday backpack special by adding some pretty lace. This no-sew project is quick, easy and timeless.

MATERIALS:

scissors
lace trim
denim backpack
  with a pocket
hot glue and
  hot glue gun

ribbon
lace fabric
denim scrap

Tip: Not into the denim and lace look? Start with a backpack in your favourite colour. Skip the bow, and use coordinating fabric to cover the pocket.

1. Cut a length of lace trim 2.5 centimetres (1 inch) longer than the backpack's pocket.

2. Turn in the raw edges of the lace 1.3 centimetres (½ inch).

3. Hot glue the lace near the top of the backpack's pocket. Glue a layer of ribbon along the pocket's edge.

4. Cut a rectangle of lace 30.5-by-22.9 centimetres (12-by-9 inches). With the right side of the lace face down, fold it into thirds.

5. Fold the short ends into the centre. Secure with a dab of hot glue.

6. Cut a 7.6-by-12.7-centimetre (3-by-5-inch) rectangle of lace. Fold in thirds along the long sides to make it 12.7-by-2.5-centimetres (5-by-1-inch). Pleat the centre of the bow and wrap the small piece of denim around the bow's centre. Glue the denim in place and reinforce bow as needed.

7. Hot glue bow to backpack.

MATERIALS:

cotton fabric in two patterns
  (one for pouch, one for lining)

0.5-m (¼-yard) lightweight
  fusible interfacing

iron

111.8 cm (44 inches) of
  2.5-cm- (1-inch-) wide cotton
  twill tape

large eyelet kit

1.3-cm (½-inch) swivel hook

hook-and-loop sticky dots

Mobile phone POCKET

Are you lost without your mobile phone?
Never feel that way again with this
lightweight, hands-free holder.

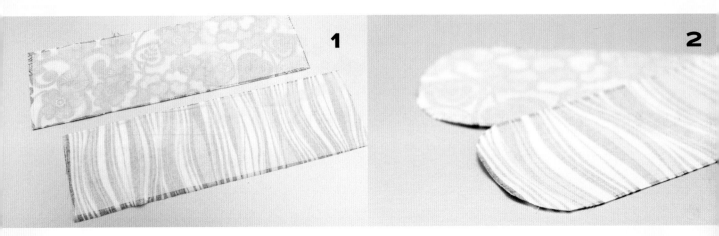

1. Cut a 10.2-by-35.6-centimetre (4-by-14-inch) rectangle from each fabric. Cut a same-size rectangle from the interfacing.

2. Use an upside-down drinking glass to trace and cut a rounded end on each of the fabric pieces.

3. Follow the instructions on the package to fuse the interface to the wrong side of the lining.

4. Pin the pouch and lining together, right-side-in. Sew around the edge in a 0.6-centimetre (¼-inch) seam, leaving a 5-centimetre (2-inch) opening on the left side.

5. Trim the corners, clip the curves and turn right-side-out. Iron.

6. Fold the pouch so that 2.5 centimetres (1 inch) of the curved ends makes a flap. This is where the eyelet will go. Line up the hook-and-loop sticky dots on the inside lining and stick on.

continued on next page

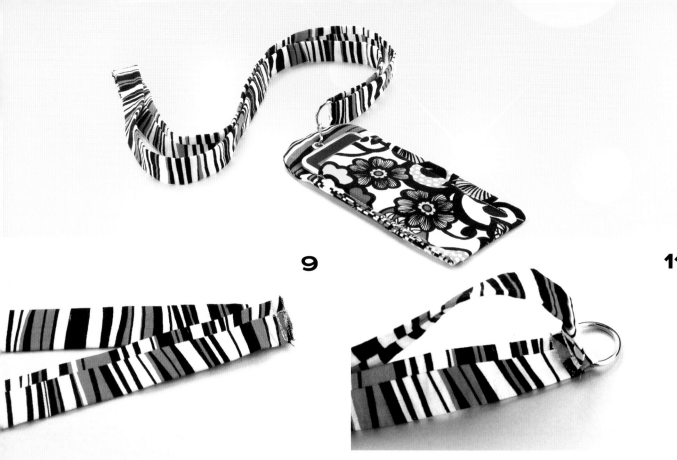

9

11

7. Fold the pouch and stitch along the edges.

8. Follow the instructions on the eyelet kit to apply the eyelet to the centre of the flap.

9. Cut a piece of fabric 111.8 centimetres (44 inches) long and 3.8 centimetres (1½ inches) wide. Fold the long edges in 0.6 centimetres (¼ inch) and sew in place to make a strap for your mobile phone pocket.

10. Slide the swivel hook into the strap and line up the two raw edges. Sew back and forth two or three times in a 1.3-centimetre (½-inch) seam. Trim the seam allowances.

11. Flip the strap so the seam is on the inside. Slide the hook down so it rests at the sewn end. Sew across the strap just above the hook to hold in place.

12. Attach the strap to the eyelet.

Tip: If you are short on interfacing, it's okay to press pieces side-by-side. Just don't overlap them or they'll make a bump in your finished piece.

MATERIALS:

paper and marker
9 cm (3.5 inch) sew-in
  purse frame
scraps of fabric
lining fabric
fusible interfacing

iron
damp cloth
needle and thread or
  sewing machine
small floral embellishment

Sweet coin PURSE

Coins rattling around in the bottom of your bag?
This project's for you! Use a sew-in clasp to make
this clever little purse.

1

Tip: Sew-in or glue-in metal purse frames are sold at craft and fabric shops.

1. To make a pattern, lay the purse frame on a sheet of plain paper and trace around the outside edge of the frame, skipping the clasp. Then draw out from the clasp's hinge to freehand the shape of your purse. Add 0.6 centimetres (¼ inch) for the seam allowance.

2. Use the pattern to cut out two purse pieces, two lining pieces and two pieces of fusible interfacing. Mark the fabric pieces with dots to show where the hinge will be on each side. Flip the pattern over to make sure everything is even. Otherwise you may end up with mismatched edges.

3. Fuse the interfacing to the wrong side of the purse pieces.

4. With the right sides together, sew the purse pieces together. Stop at the dots that mark the hinges. Repeat for the lining sections.

5. Turn the purse right-side-out. Push the lining into the purse and iron together.

6. Stitch the lining and purse together around the top edge with a 0.3-centimetre (⅛-inch) seam.

7. Push the edge of the purse into the frame and stitch in place.

8. Sew on the floral embellishment.

MATERIALS:

utility knife
old hardback book
fabric for lining
iron

2.5-cm- (1-inch-) wide
 heavyweight ribbon
wooden bag handles
hot glue and hot glue gun

Book BAG

Find an old hardback book on a library give-away shelf or at a car boot sale. Add some trendy fabric and wooden handles and transform a worn-out book into a stylish bag.

1. Use a utility knife to cut the pages from the book, leaving the cover and spine.

2. Use the open book cover to trace and cut a piece of fabric the same size. Fold and iron the edges of the fabric in 1.3 centimetres (½ inch).

3. Cut four 12.7-centimetre (5-inch) lengths of ribbon. Thread one ribbon end through the hole in the base of the bag handle. Sew the raw edges of the ribbon together. Repeat with the other three ribbons.

4. Line the handles up with the edges of the book cover. Glue the ribbons to the inside of the book cover.

5. Set the open book upright on a large piece of paper. Draw a line from the edges of the spine out to make a triangle. This will be the pattern for the sides of the bag. Add 0.6 centimetres (¼ inch) to the outside of the pattern for the seam allowance, and 2.5 centimetres (1 inch) to the height at the narrow end. Use this pattern to cut four pieces of fabric for the bag sides.

6. Sew the pairs of bag sides, right sides together, leaving a 5-centimetre (2-inch) opening. Turn and press. Hot glue the triangles to the purse sides. Hot glue the rectangle from step 2 to the inside of the book.

Tip: You can find bag handles at discount, craft and fabric shops. Choose from bamboo, leather or coloured vinyl.

MATERIALS:

two tea towels
patterned felt
pins
needle and thread or
    sewing machine
iron-on embellishments

flat-backed jewels
craft glue
5-cm- (2-inch-) wide
    cotton twill tape
    or webbing
iron

Trendy towel TOTE

Pretty tea towels are not just for drying dishes! Show off your sewing skills by turning a pair of tea towels into a terrific bag. When you see how quick and easy it is, you're going to want more than one!

1. Trim away the hemmed edges of the tea towels. If needed, trim the towels to the same size.

2. Cut around the patterns on the felt, or freehand your own. Pin them to the right side of one of the tea towels.

3. Sew the felt shapes to the towel.

4. Glue or iron on the embellishments and jewels.

5. Fold the appliqued towel in half, right-side-in, to form a bag. Sew the sides together. Repeat for the second towel.

6. Turn the outer bag (the one with the appliques) so it's right-side-out. Turn the raw edge of the bag under 1.3 centimetres (½ inch) and iron. Repeat for the second bag.

7. Slip the lining bag into the outer bag. Pin the edges together. Sew.

8. Cut two 48.3-centimetre (19-inch) lengths of twill tape. Sew in place for handles.

Tips: Medium-weight cotton tea towels work best for this project. Avoid terrycloth. Its thickness and texture make it difficult to sew.

To reinforce the handles, sew a square at the base, going through both the handle and the bag. Sew an X inside each square.

Find out more

Sewing for Kids, Alice Butcher and Ginny Farquhar
(David & Charles, 2013)

The Sewing Book, Alison Smith (Dorling Kindersley, 2009)

Unique Accessories You Can Make and Share, Mari Bolte
(Capstone Press, 2016)

About the author

Marne Ventura has written 14 Capstone books. A former primary school teacher
she holds a Master's Degree in Education from the University of California in the
United States. Marne lives with her husband on the central coast of California, USA.

Books in this series: